1

Some Frosties In a Row

By Tom Matkin

Author's Note

This is a record of an experiment I made with poetic form. The form, including meter and rhyme, I owe to Robert Frost from his masterpiece, "Stopping By Woods on a Snowy Evening". The rest is my own journey over a period of a few months. In the end I felt I had exhausted it and moved on to sonnets. Although I do still spit out the odd Frostie every now and then when that medium seems just right for the message.

This book is dedicated to Robert Frost for obvious reasons and to my wife Betty for every reason.

The Frosties

Page   Title

5

6

To Change the World

Some find their comfort in their skin
Their happiness comes from within
The blasts and roars that fly about
To such are distant, weak and dim.

Yet others look to what's without
They're sure without a single doubt
That things that matter won't be found
Exploring an internal route.

Still most I think would find it sound
To take a safer middle ground
And hedge their bets on what is best
By looking in and all around.

But if I had to choose a quest,
To change myself, or all the rest,
While either chore would be a pest,
To change the world's a stiffer test.

Cloning Around

Sometimes I'll slip into a place
To take the measure of its grace
Not knowing if I'll find it best
To give it cold or warm embrace.

I can't be sure just how I test
To see if it is cursed or blessed
These judgments merely come to me
Unconsciously I'll be impressed.

And still I never fail to see
That other's often don't agree,
They've made their judgments on their own
And see each place quite differently.

And what I find is mostly shown
Is that for me there is no clone
And when I find my comfort zone
I'm oddly often all alone.

The Man Who Golfs

The man who golfs may never know
What all that time he spent will show
Or if the effort went for naught
And merely cost him lots of dough.

Or those who like to fish a lot
And brag about the stuff they've caught
May later realize it's true
It cost too much for what they bought.

But what about those ones who do
Next to nothing. What will they rue
Content to make a great long list
Of costs a hobby might accrue?

At end of day will they be kissed
By fortunes loving fateful twist
And catch a glimpse of what they've
missed
And catch a glimpse of what they've
missed?

Streams of Life[i]

The streams of life are swift and sure
And gather us in currents pure
With little note for what we hope
As we the buffeting endure.

Oh sure! The most of us will cope
By struggling with that slippery slope
To win a trace of what we need,
Expending all our pow'r and scope.

But ought we also to concede
That streams of life don't give us heed
Whatever course we may decide
The brutal current will succeed.

Ah yes, the waves can't be denied
Our only choice: Which stream to ride!
Submission will replace our pride
Submission will replace our pride.

Bumps

I've a got a thing I like to use
It's in my car, I call it "cruise"
It's pretty easy, just to set
Then drive along, and steer and snooze.

I s'pose you'd like to make a bet
That someday I will all forget,
When driving in my silly zone,
And heap upon me great regret.

And I agree, if truth be known,
That danger clearly has been shown
To track the ones who sleep at wheel
On smooth and easy roads alone.

But lucky me, I always feel
Beneath my trusty aut'mobile
The bumps of life to keep me real,
The bumps of life to keep me real.

Stopping By

Whose bed is this I think I know
His mind is not on sleeping though
He will not see me stopping here
To watch him play his Nintendo

This little guy must think it queer
For me to watch him playing here
He races Mario 'round the lake
Most ev'ry evening of the year

I give my pocket coins a shake
To ask if there is some mistake
The only other sounds the beep
Of Warrio, that clumsy flake.

The game is lovely dark and deep
But I have promises to keep
And miles to go before I sleep
And miles to go before I sleep.

Modern Lullaby

For eighteen hours you've fought so bold
To save the world from fates untold
And gathered treasure to your heart
In calculated coins of gold.

Oh yes, you've learned the warrior's art
And kept your progress on a chart
With careful eye to fuel and pow'r
You've waged a war both strong and
smart.

And now it comes that fateful hour
When all the demons that may cower
Before your blasts of guts and gore
Will get a rest from laser shower.

While you put by your Sixty Four
And trade Nintendo for a snore
And snuggle down to sleep once more
And snuggle down to sleep once more.

I'm Feeling[ii]

I've loved and captured sweet release
From things that darkest thoughts
increase
And felt my heart and prospects soar...
But just for now, I can't find peace.

I've gathered things from off the shore
Beside the ocean's tidal roar
And filled my pockets up with stuff...
But I don't do that anymore.

I've hiked o'er lands both smooth and
rough
And stood on lonely mountain bluff
And drank the air like nectar sweet...
But at this time, it's quite enough.

I've won my share in battle's heat
And wore the victor's crown complete
But now I'm feeling full defeat
But now I'm feeling full defeat.

At War

The ships were sharing water ways
And languished there for many days
Exchanging heated battle blows
That raised a thick and acrid haze.

And each combatant boldly shows
The power of the things he knows
So proudly representing that
They come from harbours which oppose.

And so they fail to see they're at
A common point in their combat
Where enemies might better see
They've left the shores this war begat.

These ships now bravely out to sea
Could wisely cast their anchors free
And recognize the haze to be
The cause of why they can't agree.

The Wind

This wind picked up a lot of stuff
And didn't only grab the fluff!
I think the worst I heard about
Was dear old sister Mary Huff.

I s'pose at first I had a doubt
When I heard she had blown out
It isn't that the wind t'weren't strong
It's just that Mary's rather stout.

But my impression proved quite wrong
In fact, that dearie, had gone long
We found her pinned against a wall
Downwind from where we'd all belong

And bonus! Also from that squall
Lost kids and cats and cars too small,
Against that wall we found them all
Against that wall we found them all.

My New Calling

I know I never did aspire
To lead a chorus or a choir
So when I saw the bishop last
This calling didn't light my fire.

And since I'm having quite a blast
(I'm seminary early classed
And doing temple work each week)
I wondered if I ought to fast.

And see if I could maybe seek
Impressions to relieve this bleak
And unexpected choir call....
But then my conscience gave a tweak.

And I resolved to take the fall
And told the bish I'd give my all
And lead the choir while they bawl
And lead the choir while they bawl.

Suppose

Suppose your head is out of whack
Suppose you can't of things keep track
Suppose you have an awful cold
And you don't breath, you only hack.

Suppose you're taking modern mold
To try to kill the microbes bold
But still your throat's a painful fire
And you've lost hope of growing old.

Suppose you tried to lead the choir
But couldn't sing or state desire
Suppose you found your lot to be -
First shiver hard and then perspire.

If this is you then I can see
And I am sure you will agree
You're really not yourself. You're me
You're really not yourself. You're me.

Lost Hope or Guile

We tried to coax a little smile
From lips so long denied this style
And wondered if the constant frown
Was symptom of lost hope or guile.

By turning every pleasantry down
And clinging to her martyr's crown
She made a show of "in control"
That made us beggars all around.

But all this sadness took it's toll
And fewer folks tried to console
Until she sorrowed quite alone
This proud and tortured dying soul.

And by the time the end was known
It seemed her heart had turned to stone
Although, I s'pose, her fate's unknown
Although, I s'pose, her fate's unknown.

Yesterday

I'll take a pill when pain comes on
And soon the pain is usually gone
I'm not the sort to suffer when
Solutions can be easily drawn.

And though I live within my skin
And know a bit about chagrin
Sometimes a thing will go awry
That penetrates like deadly sin.

Like yesterday, I held my eye
Against the normal hazy sky
Unsure of how to take this pain
Or if I'd even live or die.

But now, today, I won't complain
I've got beyond it once again
And hardly think of what a strain
It is to suffer with migraine.

I Need Relief

No easy way or simple plan
Can match the guile of careless man
And even strategies complex
Can't stir the pot like bad luck can.

So when we fail at our projects
And thus cut off our stuck out necks
The chances are it wasn't wit
Turned optimism to perplex.

Of course there are those not legit
Who evil compacts daily knit
Such robbers cause us lots of grief
And make the streets unsafe a bit.

But while I fear and scorn the thief
I find that dumb and stupid's chief
Among the things that need relief
Among the things that need relief.

Juggling

We only reap the crop we sow
Or so the saying seems to go
And if you want it, "pay the bill"
Is good advice we all should know.

The juggler's art is practiced skill
And though it's sometimes meant to
thrill
Each one who juggles has a "best"
And won't improve by act of will.

I'm one who knows his juggling crest
Three balls for me is all I wrest
And if you add just one more ball
I'll always fail that juggling test

And juggler's watching balls that fall
Soon learn that whether large or small
When juggling orders get too tall
They don't drop one, they drop them all.

My Garden

My garden lies in silent shame
Uncertain where to place the blame
For barren earth in witness of
Our hollow hopes of harvest gain.

I'd like to place the blame above
Cause even with my gardening love
I couldn't make the garden grow
Without the bless of heaven's dove.

And since we had no water flow
Or ice or rain or even snow
From earth or sky or anywhere
Heaven's where I think the blame must
go.

Though when I find the blessings spare
That ought to come from heaven's care
I must admit what's really there....
A loving message to beware.

What Works?

Some fix their health with medicine
Some take a reading from their skin
To chase away their aches and pains
And others use a pointy pin.

Some crack their bones like endless
chains
And take a tonic for their brains
Or elixirs for gout and such
Can sometimes cause financial drains.

Still others hate a gentle touch
And like their rough massages much
While some submit to surgery
When trapped in an unhealthy clutch.

But as for me, I'd perjury
If I admitted I could see
What works in all this potpourri
What works in all this potpourri.

Taking Notice

The man would die alone in bed
No tears of sorrow would be shed
And he would be forgotten quick
As if he always had been dead.

A neighbour asks "Oh, was he sick?"
Then munching on a celery stick
She goes back to her everyday
Concerns about which show to pick.

Someone at work is in dismay
"Who's goin' to do this stuff today?"
Another thinks he might improve
And searches for his resume.

And I can't really disapprove
I'm also in my daily groove
And seldom notice those who move
And seldom notice those who move.

Go Figure

No lines on pages blessed with work
Will ever justify the smirk
That any student of the quest
Could fathom as a grand knee jerk.

And since we qualify our best
As meeting casual daily test
And leave for others no reward
Unless they show a wit possessed.

I grant the calling is restored
By asking for a sure accord
Of hearts of patience in suspense
Infused with all that we afford.

No poem should claim to recompense
As this, a lot of words, quite dense
And which, in truth, just make no sense.
And which, in truth, just make no sense.

A Modicum of Sense

There's lots of things that ought to work
But meet my try with mocking smirk
And prove my effort fruitless quest
And make me out a hopeless jerk.

And even when I do my best
To overcome life's chosen test
It seems to me that my reward
Ends up by someone else possessed.

So now for confidence restored
I'll seek to find a sure accord
And give at least some real suspense
Against results the fates afford.

And even make some recompense
By staying clear of problems dense
And using more, just common sense
And using more, just common sense.

Intertwine

A master of mahogany
He practiced wood monogamy
And wouldn't work on any tree
Without the same phylogeny.

She used to live in Tennessee
A sort of petty bourgeoisie
Who favoured oak and knotty pine
To woods of African marquee.

But now their branches intertwine
In ways described as serpentine
They took their two discordant songs
And made them one melodic line.

I wonder where such nerve belongs
And if it shortens or prolongs
This brittle world so full of wrongs
This brittle world so full of wrongs.

Consider

Consider how the rhyming verse is wrought
And with it new delights and twists of
thought
And wisdom for a small investment bought
Where sounds of pain or joy are aptly
taught.

Consider how the tongue and ear combine
To catch the genius of the words in line
And demonstrate the need to redefine
Those meanings that we formally assign.

Consider what should never be forgot,
What may in mem'ry's web be firmly caught
And must be picked apart like weaver's knot
To find and magnify our timeless lot.

Consider how the music of the rhyme
Delivered carefully in measured time
Provokes remembrance like a lasting chime
Of art and craft and hidden truth sublime.

Unhappy Men

Between unhappy men I stand
And listen to their each demand
And strive to show my open mind
So each perceives an even hand.

And sometimes I untie their bind
And leave them each one less maligned
Both satisfied with the affair
And points of view now realigned.

But such an end is very rare
And probably will need repair
When time and worry have their way
Restoring what they thought unfair.

Thus justice brings me much dismay
And of the usual case I'll say
Unhappy men just stay that way
Unhappy men just stay that way.

Any Path

An ancient walk from garden way
Foreshadowed paths in latter day
Where each would leave his first estate
Because he could no longer stay.

We know some came at early date
And other's held until quite late
And some by painful twisted way
While other's paths were smooth and
straight.

So I'm content in my delay
To be here in a happier day
Than when the truth was lost from men
And every path in disarray.

But maybe in that "garden", then,
I so looked forward to my "when"
That any path won my amen
That any path won my amen.

The Stage

It thunders out through every age
That blackened thing we call the stage
Assaulting every sense of those
Who choose its powers to engage.

And sitting in the first few rows
Each confidante of nightly shows
Is blessed or shattered in his place
By questions which the play may pose.

And as the stage seems to erase
Such disbelief as threatens grace
I've come to love its masquerade
And marvel at its double face.

And when the scene is just-right played
And my perceptions all betrayed
I hope the lights will never fade
I hope the lights will never fade.

Two Voices: First Voice

I see you're full of love and hope
I know it's how you try to cope
But as for me I'm not that way
I can't believe beyond this scope.

I don't expect a brighter day
All heroes just have feet of clay
And no one ever rescued me
Or answered when I bowed to pray.

I see you there on bended knee
I even hear your fervent plea
But please don't push that pie in sky
On folks like me who just can't see.

To me it's clear we can't rely
On miracles from up on high
We live, we suffer, then we die
We live, we suffer, then we die.

Two Voices: Second Voice

I've built my life from hope to hope
It goes beyond the need to cope
I'm sure there is no other way
I cannot limit heaven's scope.

My faith has brightened every day
And rescued me from out the clay
It's such a saving gift for me
I have to bow in thanks and pray.

And so I'm here on bended knee
And make my fervent hopeful plea
To Him who rules us from the sky
I beg for Him to help you see.

That you may know you can rely
On miracles from up on high
From birth, until the day you die
From birth, until the day you die.

Hey Poindexter! Git Yerself a Rhymin'
Dictionary

I figgered out to write a verse
A lovely one that's not too worse
A dictionary really helps;
A rhyming one, right in yer purse.

Cuz then you can find words like yelps
Or rhyme with helps by using phelps
It's almost endless what will work
Take seaweed, you could call it kelps.

And if I go a bit berserk
And I don't mean that clean and jerk
I mean to say my verse is nice
And written with a proper smirk.

If you want rhyming words precise
I recommend you pay the price
Five dollars should about suffice
Five dollars should about suffice.

Her Passage

Each breath is shallow, short and tight
A symptom of her gloom and fright
And every passing minute shows
She's moving further from the light.

And as her private darkness grows
She hopes this agony will close
And build a veil to shield her mind
Against the things she thinks she knows.

But bitter ashes still remind
Her of the peace she could not find
In faithless, barren, selfish quest
Down streets and alleys proven blind.

I hope her passage now is blessed,
And comfort settles in her breast...
She found no gladness in this test
She found no gladness in this test.

His Final Test

He holds the pistol still and tight
And tries to will away his fright
Embarrassed that his aspect shows
Such terror in this summer light.

And as his apprehension grows
His curious eyes he tries to close
To shut this scene from out his mind
And think of happier things he knows.

But other senses still remind
That he will not in this life find
The product of his peaceful quest
Among the angry and the blind.

His mission and his works are blessed,
And witness settles in my breast
That he will pass this final test
That he will pass this final test.

Wounded

I stubbed my toe the other day
And then my tongue got in the way
Of teeth enjoined by elbows thrown
Into my chin along the way.

I sneezed a fit from some cologne
Worn by some person quite unknown
And my eyes watered through and
through
From second hand smoke at me blown.

And my girlfriend bid me adieu
(I didn't have the slightest clue)
And then my dog he up and died
And someone stole my prize canoe.

And all of this I took in stride
But there's a pain I cannot hide
It's when I'm wounded in my pride
It's when I'm wounded in my pride.

The Sandman Cometh

The great and mighty high greased
leader
Assigned some one to be the reader
Then sat among his white haired friends
And slept as quiet as a cedar.

The worthy ward cluck put his pens
Beside his bag of odds and ends
And laid his head into his hands
And slept as gladly as his friends.

The demon deacon understands
The magic of the ceiling fans
And as he stares they hypnotize
Until he's safe in day dream lands.

And the dry council still supplies
A potent cure for open eyes...
The sandman in a church disguise
The sandman in a church disguise.

I Tried to Speak

I picked some verse to write for you
I chose it carefully and true
And then I typed it on a page
And added just a word or two.

I've sometimes hoped my verse was sage
Just needing, like fine wine, to age
Or even thought it might be song
And suited well for center stage.

But with my rhyme and meter wrong
And notions neither pure nor strong
So lightly forged without technique
It's clear that's not where they belong.

No matter if your find it weak
And lacking imagery unique
At least, this once, I tried to speak
At least, this once, I tried to speak.

The firstest frostie

The firstest frostie that I writ
Tied me up tight like in a fit
The rhythm and the rhymin' stuff
Made this ol' cowboy want to quit.

And so becuz it was so ruff
I soon had had more than enuff
And didn't try again for days
Preferring lim'rick powder puff.

But when I'd come outta my daze
And cleared away my rhymin' haze
I still could not shake off the need
To try ta start a frostie craze.

Then finally I did succeed
And now what once was just a seed
Is growing freely like a weed
Is growing freely like a weed.

Newsmakers

Who makes the news I sometimes ask
It seems a hard and thankless task
To be the source of what we know
Of how our neighbor's trials unmask.

Who gets to be the foil to show
Each hit's a universal blow
And each man's pain is also mine...
Who gets to pose for that tableau?

I guess it's all done by design
No one may offer, or decline.
It has to be that way I guess
Or every maker would resign.

So I give thanks to such as bless
Us with a show of their distress
And pray I'm never in that mess
And pray I'm never in that mess.

Remember When I Was a Prince?

Remember once I got it right?
Oh yeah! I hear I nailed it tight...
I just forget just what it was
That gave me such a great delight.

Remember when I heard applause
For pirouettes danced without flaws?
I'm just afraid I don't recall
Dance steps I've made except faux pas.

Remember when I stood so tall
And people called me "on the ball"?
A lot of things have happened since
To make my reputation small.

Remember when I was a prince?
It's not that easy to convince
That my nod ever made men wince
That my nod ever made men wince.

The Mountain in the Lake

I look across the quiet lake
To where the shore and water break
And see the woods and mountain peak
Converging there like some mistake.

I try to understand this streak
And wish it had a way to speak
To share the secrets that it knows
And help me find the peace I seek.

It has to hold a key to those
Illusions that we can't expose
And separate a scene that's true
From shadows which we just suppose.

One day I'll kneel in my canoe
And float out past horizon's view
And bid this questioning adieu
And bid this questioning adieu.

Angry Birthday Cake[iii]

A piece of angry birthday cake
A challenge that was no mistake
No easy sort of tinder box
A cruel, empty kind of snake.

A headless animal that talks
Or water sifting out of rocks
And captured clouds in ancient days
Like bagels eaten without lox.

Give up your purple stolen ways
And reach inside this solemn phrase
For as the seed can't cast its rind
Your life's cemented into plays.

Such images don't bless your mind
They're false and foolish and unkind
They promise insight, but just blind
They promise insight, but just blind.

The Trend

I hope it only rains at night
And that the sun is shining bright
Between the morn and evening stars
Without a cloud to hide the light.

I want my lessons without scars
No bogies for me, only pars
And I can't look for what you need
My focus is on "mine" not "ours".

I want my garden without weed
And in a group, I want to lead
Perhaps you want me as a friend?
I'll think about it, if you'll plead.

I 'spect one day I'll comprehend
Why what I do seems to offend
But as for now, that's not the trend
But as for now, that's not the trend.

Stopping Between Rounds On a Snowy Evening

Whose woods are these? I ought to know.
That putter ain't familiar though
And all those bags of clubs right here
Should be removed in case of snow.

My playing partner thinks it's queer
To stop without a clubhouse near
Between the caddy shack and lake
This coldest golf day of the year.

He gives his pocket change a shake
Then ponies up for his mistake
And watches as the caddies sweep
The cart shed clean of every flake.

The practice green is dark and deep
But I've a foursome date to keep
And holes to play before I sleep
And holes to play before I sleep.

Shrimp for Lunch

I think some shrimp for lunch is nice....
(I like it when it's on crushed ice
Although I've had some deep fat fried
Which goes real well with greens and
rice.

Another thing I've often tried
Is steak with shrimp that's stuffed inside
I hear that Neptune eats this way
A flavor famous worldwide.

Of course I could eat everyday
Alfredo as they like to say
With lots of heavy cream and cheese
And noodles and some shrimp at play.

And then there's shrimp in Cantonese
Or Szechwan stir fry cooked with peas...)
I think .... some shrimp for my lunch
please
I think .... some shrimp for my lunch
please.

Chalk Up One for Me

I wonder when my time is up
What will be said about this pup
If what I've done will fill a pail
Or barely splash into a cup?

Yeah, what will be the sort of scale
That will be used to give detail
To how I've crossed the seas of time...
A tiny minnow or a whale?

Perhaps it would not be a crime
To lend a hand in verse and rhyme
By listing of my humble span
Some thing I've done that's quite sublime.

Among the best, since I began
Though 'twasn't really done by plan
I've just installed a ceiling fan
I've just installed a ceiling fan.

Walking on a June Morning

The narrow light that streaks along
The paths and fields of morning song
Unlike the brighter eyes of noon
Detects what's been congealed in wrong.

One seldom thinks of flaws in June
While hope and brightness play their
tune
And shadows at the dawn of light
Most always are forgotten soon.

These vivid shades, remnants of night
Remind that there is black and white
And though the day may burst with
flowers
The dark is only out of sight.

I like to walk these early hours
And study these contrasting powers
And watch as light the night devours
And watch as light the night devours.

Measuring Time

We wave our arms and pound our feet
And snap our fingers to the beat
We sometimes sing the count out loud
When there's no need to be discreet.

At times the pace is firm and proud
And other times it's... like a cloud
But every song has its tempo
Though deviations are allowed.

And every life sways to and fro
Sometimes real quick... and sometimes slow
We waver between slack and prime
From quiet nod to tapping toe.

So it's by rhythm and by rhyme
That hearts beat out our fall and climb
Each life's a song that measures time
Each life's a song that measures time.

Oh Bother

I'd like to take a trip. A quest.
And thereby add a little zest
To what is such a simple life
It hardly seems a proper test.

I wouldn't need a drum and fife
Just heavy shoes and pocket knife
And X marked on a parchment map
To give direction to my strife.

And maybe, a kind, friendly chap
The sort that wears a silly cap
To share adventures on the road
And watch for danger while I nap.

Oh, yes, we'd talk in secret code
And then in modest hero mode
I'd find that X, the mother lode,
And take it back to my abode.

Behind the Clouds

The sun went back to work today
Because the rain went on its way
And things began to heat and grow
And kids and pets came out to play.

I often ask, "Where does it go?"
That trusty sun, in rain and snow
I wonder if it stays in place
Or takes a rest... how could we know?

I know if something hides my face
I sometimes show a change of pace
Or wander down beside the creek
And take a day or two of grace.

And so I'd like to take a peek
Behind the clouds some rainy week
And watch the sun play hide and seek
And watch the sun play hide and seek.

On Fresh and Easy Morning Wind

On fresh and easy morning wind
A host of foolish hopes are pinned
We always feel the better part
Before our day is stained and sinned.

We take false courage at the start
And lunge and rush with noble heart
As if our lives were exercised
Like anaerobic works of art.

But then our virtue's compromised
Our plans are once again revised
And as the end of day draws near
Our disappointment's undisguised.

Still, soon, a new tomorrow's here,
With soothing breeze to melt our fear,
And forge the faith to persevere
And forge the faith to persevere.

Tenderhearted

Those practiced gentle kindly arts
Of trusting and of generous hearts
May seem a weak and feeble force
Compared to harsh and fiery darts.

Those things refined and never coarse
That keep the pureness of the source
Are ridiculed and boldly knocked
By those who deal in cold remorse.

Those pastures which are never locked
Where peace abundantly is stocked
And love and softness overdone,
By natural men are roundly mocked.

I choose the tenderhearted run
And take my strength d'rect from the
sun
Not from the pow'r of sword or gun
Not from the pow'r of sword or gun.

Portrait of Christ by Kelly Davis

The kindly eyes and patient face
Are sketched with an uncommon grace
Not often caught by one so young....
I'll hang it in a special place.

Sometimes even what we've sung
Or uttered with a practiced tongue
Is faint beside a picture's power....
I see now where it should be hung.

Between the lovely temple's tower
And holy prophet for this hour
The Lord of life and death should reign....
Here, let's take down that tired flower.

This art does more than entertain
A sign of every parent's pain...
And comfort that we can't explain
And comfort that we can't explain.

Perpetual Motion

When I think of that buttered bun
And how it tumbled, just for fun
It brings a tear into my eye
With hopes of tidy lunch undone.

But I won't only sit and cry
I'll heave a resignated sign
And think about my coming test
As I my lunchtime soon will try.

It's ever such a sacred quest
To keep a clean unsullied vest
For those like me, who're giv'n to fat
And who their butter fingers best.

I think what's brewing in my hat...
I'll save from floor and vest this pat
By spreading butter on my cat
By spreading butter on my cat.

More Perpetual Motion

That cat might smear a butter pat
Upon the vest or shirt of hat
But one thing we can say for sure
Upon the floor. No back of cat.

And here's another sort of cure
For messes cats will oft procure
It has to do with using toast
To keep that butter clean and pure.

Because it's not an idle boast
That buttered toast will never coast
Onto the floor with butter up
A floor will only greaseside host.

So when it's time for you to sup
Don't put yer butter in a cup
Just toast it on your feline pup
Just toast it on your feline pup.

In Time

The man fell in the sewer young
Before his reason had begun
The filth and germs have had their way
And now his soul's replaced with dung.

So even if we wash away
The surface and the plain decay
What's hidden in his deeper parts
Will spread that muck and its bouquet.

So what to do with foul hearts
Who suffer by their fallen starts
And harbor evil growing slime
And spread it thick with all their arts?

Some advocate a pit of lime
To 'radicate the world from grime
And that's what some will get, in time
And that's what some will get, in time.

I Think

I think therefore I think I am
My own inbox is boxed with spam
I have a taste for tasty meals
Of angel cake and deviled ham.

I'm stepping on my rundown heels
I'm rolling on my wheeler deals
And one with only common cents
Can't change my touch or how it feels.

The milk of kindness won't condense
Or make a neighbor buy a fence
Unless those words of wisdom true
Are lost in past and present tense.

There's things I will or will not do
To say no more nor less than you
As I cook words up in a stew
As I cook words up in a stew.

Don't Think About it Over Much

Don't think about it over much
When you are in the devil's clutch
Don't waste your effort on a plan
It can't be fixed with thinking's touch.

It's been the same since time began
When evil knocked, he shudda ran
To stay and reason with the creep
Has been the downfall of the man.

There's times we ought to look, not leap
And ponder while we eat and sleep
There's times it's best to slowly seek
For answers that are wise and deep.

But there's no time for that technique
When Satan gets you cheek to cheek
Just turn your back and make a streak
Just turn your back and make a streak.

Night Night

It's getting late out here at last
What once was future, now is past
And if I look upon the clock
I see it all went by too fast.

I only meant to check the lock
And see what email was in stock
But then I thought I'd write one verse ...
And now, the time! Oh, what a shock.

I suppose I cudda been more terse
And then again, perhaps, much worse
There's still an hour or so before
I reach that fateful midnight curse.

But most aren't with me anymore
No longer bothered by this bore
They've settled for their nightly snore
They've settled for their nightly snore.

Questions that Demand Answers

And what's so wrong with perfect hair?
Is it a sin to comb with care?
Let's give a cheer for those with class
Who fix their hair beyond compare.

And what's so wrong with perfect grass?
Is it a sin when lawns surpass?
Let's give a cheer for those who groom
Their lawns and gardens first and last.

And what's so wrong with fine perfume?
Is it a sin to scent a room?
Let's give a cheer for those who smell
As sweet as flowers in their bloom.

And after life, where will they dwell?
Those perfect ones who so excel?
Do you hope they're in perfect hell?
Do you hope they're in perfect hell?

The Trouble with Lions

I found a lion in my yard
It wasn't really very hard
He roared, I think, throughout the night
And gave our sleeping no regard.

Still, otherwise, he was polite
And came inside at my invite,
Right off we had a lovely race
And only stopped to tease and fight.

We played our simple game of chase
Until we knocked down mother's vase
And then she sternly made us sit
In kitchen corner, face to face.

We didn't really want to quit
But she made each of us admit
That we were reckless, just a bit
That we were reckless, just a bit.

Confused

I wandered lonely as a cloud
Is beautiful to say out loud
And when he read it to his friends
I'm sure it made old Wordsworth proud

I took the one least traveled by
May seem a loner to imply
But I hear Robert Frost could talk
For hours to almost any guy.

To be or not to be may be
The thing to ponder over tea
And we've all heard it said this way
Because of Shakespeare's tragedy.

It's sad a little, in a way
That what these genius poets say
Has now become, in modern day
Confused, by many, with cliché.

Hand of Fate

The hard and lasting hand of fate
May make a change to your estate
At any time or any place
Without a warning or debate.

It may all pretenses erase
And introduce you to disgrace
And fill your cup with bitterness
At lightening speed, or casual pace.

Or sometimes fate will warmly bless
With unexpected tenderness.
These things don't happen every day,
The things that strengthen or distress.

But still we feel their constant stay
It's not that they return to play
It's that they never go away
It's that they never go away.

The Artful Shrill

One should not fear the frightful scold
So nasty, terrible and bold,
Such cannot win a victim's trust
Or force a fickle heart to hold.

One has to doubt the forceful thrust
Of power exercised like lust
That flaunts its strong and iron will
And deals in currency of "must".

A study of the artful shrill
Exposes that it cannot kill
Or ever capture any soul
That will not yield before its skill.

It makes a pretext of control
Intimidation is the goal
There is no fire in that hole
There is no fire in that hole.

Early Spring

The power of the warming sun
Finds work enough that's still undone
And sets to make the world grow
And ice bound streams begin to run.

So we forget the winter snow
As splendid green begins to show
And promise of a brighter day
Is felt as rainy breezes blow.

Such hope is couched in this array
Of springtime flowers and all at play
That fairly every heart will sing
And joy and laughter claim the way.

But then, sometimes, the phone will ring
And news that changes everything
Will put an early end to spring
Will put an early end to spring.

Have a Heart

I heard they put another heart
In someone not named Barney Clark
It's made of wire and plastic things
And looks a lot like modern art.

With metal motor and small springs
A battery and some o-rings
And through the skin 'lectric transmit
To charge it up. I'll bet that stings!

Before you qualify for it
Your heart must be declared unfit
It must be on it's final phase
They must be sure it's soon to quit.

It's hard to give this project praise
It promises to only raise
Expectancy by 30 days
Expectancy by 30 days.

A Way of Life

Suppose you have a broken wrist
Low blood, high temp, or pilar cyst
Or if your stomach acid's high
You're sure to see a pharmacist.

These wizards have a great supply
Of pills and such to keep you spry
Or slow you down so you don't care
That something in your life's awry.

And now, in case we're unaware
Commercials fill the broadcast air
Across the world the TV's rife
With druggist's ads of healing fare.

And thus from birth to end of strife
Between assaults from surgeon's knife
Our medicine's a way of life
Our medicine's a way of life.

Blood

What sort of blood do you prefer;
reptilian or under fur?
I think the kind that's warm is nice
and hope that you will all concur.

I'm glad my veins don't run with ice
Or track the ambient precise,
to keep from havin' blood too thin
I b'lieve I'd pay a pretty price.

Some critters, those with scaly skin,
have blood that doesn't heat within
they have to find a sunny spot
to keep from gettin' cold as sin.

And come that day when I am not
and all my flesh has gone to rot
I'll still be pleased my blood was hot
I'll still be pleased my blood was hot.

Quaking Aspens

My neighbor planted aspen trees
The ones with lovely quaking leaves
To shade his deck and house from sun
And catch the early evening breeze.

And soon their roots began to run
And trees popped up where I had none,
At first I mowed and cut them back
And then I let one grow, for fun.

Now I have trees all 'round my shack
And though I tug and pull and hack
The roots shoot up new starts each day;
My garden's under full attack.

I s'ppose if I would cut away
Those aspens I've allowed to stay
Then I could keep the roots at bay
Then I could keep the roots at bay.

We Babbled[iv]

Remember when we babbled on
We talked at midnight, noon and dawn
We shared, we argued and we chattered
Though most conclusions were foregone.

It's not as if it really mattered
Our logic often somewhat tattered
As we discussed the daily scene
It wasn't focused, it was scattered.

Still we each had our own routine
Some were happy, some were mean
Some were sappy, some absurd
And some were kind, and some extreme.

But now we hardly speak a word
Still friends, I guess, but nothing's heard
I think I know why this occurred
I think I know why this occurred.

Desire

If snakes were sleeping in your bed
And crawling round your neck and head
You wouldn't try to learn their charms
You'd change the place you sleep instead.

When you hear sirens or alarms
That warn of deadly fire or harms
You take those warnings to your heart
Like any other call to arms.

It isn't ever really smart
To toss around a poisoned dart
You know what that will make transpire
That's why you wouldn't even start.

Still worse than snakes and darts and
fire
Are things with consequences dire
We do to gratify desire
We do to gratify desire.

Misconstrued

She swaggers down the runway ramp
Then stops and does her practiced vamp
And then too soon to catch her eye
She's back inside the model's camp.

She changes outfits on the fly
And someone's there to help supply
New make-up, hair... or fix what may
Have in her changing gone awry.

Then down the ramp for more display
Another dress, another way
Another look, another mood,
Another style, another day....

While some may find these rituals lewd
Our model isn't such a prude
She knows her art is misconstrued
She knows her art is misconstrued.

Legacies of Pain

It's clear the climber has a dream
Then tries to execute his scheme.
What gives him courage to decide
To make his pathway so extreme?

It must be something deep inside
Some power usually denied
That drives him to the very brink
Where vanity and life collide.

This bravery is fine, I think
But doing what could in a blink
Unforge a climber's lifelong chain
Demands a far more noble link.

What does a selfish climber gain
By dying young in life's campaign
And leaving legacies of pain
And leaving legacies of pain?

Playing Pioneer

Those pioneers were hardy types
I s'ppose they had their share of gripes
But due to what they suffered through
I'm sure they musta won their stripes.

I rode a covered wagon too
I sat up high, enjoyed the view,
I fixed a harness, fed a mule
And helped a vet nail on a shoe.

For me it was a sort of school
My effort at the golden rule
To empathize with ancestors
Who suffered deprivations cruel.

And though I did a week of chores
I'm 'fraid we come from diff'rent shores
And each must fight his private wars
And each must fight his private wars.

Out of Obscurity

He swings the heavy two-edged ax
So hard, he comes up from his tracks
And as it crosses rays of sun
The flashing blade marks all his hacks.

This farmer's son has just begun
Each tree he falls, a vict'ry won
And every blow a battle fought
To make this darkness come undone.

He hopes to claim a homestead plot
In nature's sylvan fingers caught
And leave a meadow clean and pure
Embroidered with a thick wood lot.

This forest grove may be obscure
The axeman young, and very poor
And time will test. But he'll endure.
And time will test. But he'll endure.

Thanksgiving

One farmer casts his seed abroad
You see the pattern where he's trod
To spread upon the furrowed plain
The start of new productive sod.

It may not be in his domain
To water newly planted grain
Another one may tend the shoots
And see they get their share of rain.

Then as the plantings put out roots
Another yet may harvest fruits,
By now the planter's long forgot
And turned to different pursuits.

I s'ppose a harvest from a plot
That we have pers'n'lly sown not
Should bring thanksgiving - quite a lot
Should bring thanksgiving - quite a lot.

In Plastic[v]

When in the course of daily life
Your pet succumbs to age or strife
What will you do with Tabby's bod
Now he's as stiff as poor Lot's wife?

Don't make a mess out of your sod
By turning up a backyard clod
And don't you buy a plot for pet
And thereby shoot a tidy wad.

And to placate your pet regret
Don't burn him like a cigarette.
I know a way that's not too drastic,
And you will like it too, I bet.

Just say a word ecclesiastic
Then wrap your favourite pet in plastic
And throw him in the dump. Fantastic!
And throw him in the dump. Fantastic!

Dancing With Sacred Cows

We got those letters back in France
The one's where strangers asked to dance
But we could not allow it then
And had to shun their knowing glance.

I wondered as I took my pen
To write "no thank you" to those men
How such a trouble came to be
And if I'd hear from them again.

Ten years or more I'd have to see
Before the word came back to me
That every one was welcome now
Essentially, the dance was free.

We still may sometimes wonder how
This practice that we now allow
Became, for some, a sacred cow
Became, for some, a sacred cow.

Reflections on Alma 12:11

Behold the proud and guilty mind
Endowed with special notions blind
Bereft of reason, and of luck
His trade is murmurings refined.

Don't question stamina or pluck
Although on one-note he is stuck
He works and struggles day by day
To paper over all his muck.

I don't suppose it's mine to say
But wisdom tells me those who stray
Will get come uppance in the end
Perhaps when turned back into clay.

Till then, how low will he descend?
As if compelled, he must contend.
It hurts to see this in a friend
It hurts to see this in a friend.

Elbow Grease and Style

I asked around, I bought a book
I found some samples, took a look
I schemed and planned and thought a lot
And guessed what money this work took.

And when I had the plan I'd sought
And felt I knew what I might wrought
I started in the toughest part
To get my wife to share my thought.

For since her judgment's pretty smart
I knew I shouldn't even start
To fix our bathroom shower while
We were not of a common heart.

Then adding elbow grease and style
We both applied ceramic tile
And now we shower with a smile
And now we shower with a smile.

Virtual Zest

The ancient history of the 'net
Is measured not in years I'll bet
A post that's over 2 days old
Is like the fossil record - set.

Perhaps that's why there's much of bold
And precious few the posts of gold
When discourse races like the wind
The point's forgot before it's cold.

And worse that most for content thinned
Are po-ems very quickly spinned
I know this cuz I'm guiltiest
By vapid rapid verse I've sinned.

So while I seldom do my best
At least I write with virtual zest
To get things quickly off my chest
To get things quickly off my chest.

Auto Pilot Breakdown

The functions that we need the most
To help our bodies run, not roast
Are automatic generally
And work just fine from coast to coast.

But now and then we sadly see
Controlling factors twirling free
And temperatures and other things
Like wastes and fluids (not on knee).

Producing crises nature brings
To men and women, bums and kings
That's when we turn to medicine
And pray the praises heaven sings.

What is it? Germs, disease or sin
That makes my head and stomach spin
At least I'm sure it isn't gin
And in the end, I'll be more thin.

Worthy Quest

To ski the highest wild slopes
Above and far beyond the ropes
Takes just the sort of fearlessness
That's only found among real dopes.

To dare to bungee with finesse
Or sharks and crocodiles caress
Is something to be proud about
For those who value stupidness

To roar around a racing route
Or get into a boxing bout
Defies the senses of the wise
And makes them want to scream and
shout.

Is there no real and worthy quest
No actual maidens in distress
That blind men must climb Everest
That blind men must climb Everest?

It Takes a Lickin' in August

All hail the king of summer fun
The cooling sweet delicious one
The answer to the question of
How do you beat the summer sun?

Those sticks they fit it like a glove
Those sticks, those sticks! I'm so in love,
A treat beyond the normal fare
A treat that's from the up above.

If I ate one in church, they'd stare
So I can't have them everywhere
But still, desire isn't fickle
I want them all the time, I swear.

Oh yes, far better than a pickle
And costing 'bout a double nickle
All hail the wonderful popsicle
All hail the wonderful popsicle.

Those Science Guys

Archemedes, what a chump
He put all pastry in the dump
His pie, while quite precise you see
Would never serve much more than
three.

And Alyhazar he was clear
That water bent the light that's near
So sticks may stand, but never straight
When stirring drinks or dangling bait.

And old Pythagorus I know
Saw triangles where ere he'd go
But squares like him should never try
To measure hippopotami.

And what about that cute Bill Nye
The one they call the science guy
He tries to make it all seem simple
Then grins and shows his teeth and
dimple.

Of Trees and Men

The root of life is what you know
It's wisdom helps the sapling grow
And holds the giant tree in place
Against the wind and ice and snow.

The limbs of life are love and grace
To shield, extend, and give embrace
They offer shade, and catch the sun
By reaching high t'ward heaven's face.

The fruit of life it what you've done
Each service given one by one
In season, and in each pursuit
Until your final race is run.

Some trees will thrive without much root
And others barely raise a shoot
But none would last without the fruit
But none would last without the fruit.

At the Well

Where ever desert people dwell
Not far from where they buy and sell
And where the village center lies...
An ordinary water well.

So precious what this font supplies
It represents an equal prize
To traveler or native son,
Indigenous or foreign eyes.

And we may read that brides are won
And ways of wantonness undone
And of the angels leading on
The wretched from the dark to sun.

When this well water has been drawn
Great blessings can be poured upon
Each one whose worldly hopes are gone
Each one whose worldly hopes are gone.

Correcting Others

I've sometimes wished my mind could dance
In never-ending light romance
And blind with drool and witty sense
The boring grasp of happenstance.

I've wished my genius was immense
For baring tiresome pretense
By happy light and airy verse
And jests that never give offense.

I want the power to converse
So that the precious and perverse
Will realize their woeful state
Yet still not think of me the worse.

But I must sadly now relate
Correcting others through debate
Has only made them more irate
Has only made them more irate.

Teachin' Cows ta Dance[vi]

You've gotta teach yer cows to dance
It'll never happen just by chance
A herd that's not instructed will
Just waste its days, as if in trance.

Some like ta start 'em with a thrill
With heart throb dances from Brazil
So then the cows will practice when
They have some extra time to kill.

But others start with basic steps
So all their cows are waltz adepts
Instead of learning Latin beats...
Each simple move, a million reps.

When teachin' cows it's always neat
To help 'em learn to lift their feet
A dancing cow that steps real high
Brings everyone out of his seat.

I've seen 'em give line-dance a try
With "Achy Breaky" on the fly
They'll kick and shuffle to and fro
Each cow a slappin' hoof and thigh.

But ballroom dancin's apropos
For cows who really feel the flow
A dip, a whirl, the swish of silk
Those waltzin' cows can really go!

Still dancin' and things of that ilk
Are, in the end, just so much bilk
What cows do best is give us milk
What cows do best is give us milk.

We Whisper

We whisper in a whisp'ring crowd
Rehearsing what we've just avowed
As strangers in a sacred place
We never speak these things aloud.

These moments transcend time and
space
And endless happiness embrace
Evoking sanctifying love,
To sin and loneliness erase.

Recorded here and up above
Each passage not just symbols of
The destiny of every one
When casting off this earthly glove.

It seems we've only just begun ...
But now the ceremony's done
Come marvel at the freedom won
Come marvel at the freedom won.

Curry Garlic Fudge

I favour curry garlic fudge
That chocolate stuff is just plain sludge
But there's no way to figure taste
Each person is his own best judge.

I like my exercise slow paced
To break a sweat... I'd feel disgraced
But you may find aerobics fun
Where I think it's a total waste.

And I won't ever shoot a gun
You stop and fight, I'll turn and run
I know some people disapprove
But lots of them were early done.

What all these contradictions prove?
Is just how hard it is to move
With each so stuck in his own groove
With each so stuck in his own groove.

In the Drink

You set the drunkard on the pier
And aim him carefully for fear
He'll stagger off into the drink
Before he gets into the clear.

You catch him constantly and think
Why is he always on the brink?
He cannot seem to find the path
To save himself from certain sink.

And worse your efforts draw his wrath
He seems determined for his bath
And safety doesn't phase the pup
He just can't seem to do the math.

And so you finally leave the schulp
Resigned that till he sobers up
He'll have to drink his bitter cup.
He'll have to drink his bitter cup.

With What's Left

Oh, teach me, cruel circumstance
Destroy me like a game of chance
Expose my weaknesses to fire
And burn me with your flaming glance.

Eradicate what I desire
Keep from me what I might acquire
And rend my proud self centered soul
A weak and feeble, beaten, liar.

Deflect my footsteps from my goal
Release me from all self control
And with what's left, if anything,
Build up a man who's wise and whole.

I must withstand the brutal sting
Of everything this world can bring
If I would be a priest and king
If I would be a priest and king.

If He Won't Quit

I think the devil may have tried
In vain to have me vilified
I hope his efforts slacken now
I'd be real great if they'd subside.

I hope he knows I've figured how
To watch with hand upon the plough
And that he's lost all hope at last
That I will ever disavow.

It seems that I've been so harassed
By temptations quite unsurpassed
That he should be exhausted by
His efforts now and in the past.

One thing that seems to catch my eye
About this battle that we vie:
If he won't quit, then nor will I
If he won't quit, then nor will I.

Don't Ask

She asked if we would drive until
We got to Texas or Brazil
Or must she wait for my collapse
Then ask the way against my will?

She asked me if I thought perhaps
Before another week's elapse
It might be wise to take a glance
At one or more of all our maps?

These notions made the briefest dance
Inside my hunter's stubborn trance
Then frozen out by manly pride
They vanished like a snowball's chance.

Don't ask directions on a ride
Until you've every pathway tried
And never sooner than you've died
And never sooner than you've died.

Some Worshipers

Some worshipers bow to the east
And so for such, a worthy priest,
Must keep a compass close at hand
To orient their prays, at least.

Some pilgrims seek a holy land
On hills, or plains or desert sand
They need to find a promised place
To meet their spiritual demand.

Some seekers concentrate on grace
And glory how it will erase
Their every sin or weakness 'til
They meet their maker face to face.

Still others look to sweat and skill
Integrity and force of will,
They put their shoulders to the wheel
And hope their works will fill the bill.

True rites and rigors are ideal
And good works help cement the deal
But only grace and mercy heal
But only grace and mercy heal.

Mockery

To mock the kids who play at chess
And value academic-ness
Is just the sort of crazy sport
Some dopes can play with great finesse.

Nor should the academic sort
Make fun of those who rule the court.
And still, there's some who don't excel
They always seem to come up short.

We'd like to think each one does well
At something. But the truth to tell
As objects ripe for laughing at
There lots of us who come off swell.

I'll let ya know in nothin' flat
As soon as I get it down pat,
The way to deal with all of that
And not be hurt by every brat.

Each Moment

No cell phone call will come his way
No pager message clouds his day
He takes each moment as a gift
Not thinking if it's work or play.

No one describes his mind as "swift"
Or makes a fuss about his thrift
The market doesn't interest him
He isn't driven. He's adrift.

He moves about from whim to whim
His prospects best described as "slim"
And while he's pleasant on the whole
He's oft accused of wits too dim.

Still, he's a loyal, friendly, soul
And plays a certain useful role
And wags his tail beyond control
And wags his tail beyond control.

Playing Scales

The sound you hear is me at play
That drumming cadence of cliche
With rhythm and with choking rhyme
I learn this craft while on display.

The voice is earnest, most the time,
The meter over true, not fine
Just beaten out like music scales
It's repetitious by design.

Few thoughtful, moving, poignant tales
Emerge when practicing prevails
Still even as I do this drill
Sometimes a melody unveils.

These poems are like a flour mill
Monotonous and worn and shrill
Refining endlessly a skill
Refining endlessly a skill.

In Between

Not tossed aside or left behind
Not in a place I couldn't find
But gone. But good. And far and long.
It's real. Not just a state of mind.

Where once were voices raised in song
Where once we two were like one strong
What now? A cold and empty hand?
It's real. Where now, do I belong?

I saw our footprints in the sand
I saw us, partners in this land
Look now. The tide has washed it clean!
It's real. I saw, we dreamed, we planned.

And what's the purpose of this scene,
And what do all these shadows mean?
Why me? The one left in between
Why me? The one left in between.

Swans are Everything, Everything I Wish I Could Be

I'll bet a day will come some time
When swans will be considered prime
When long necked birds will rule the roost
And man will be in deep decline.

With human influ'nce thus reduced
Economies will get a boost
And green house gasses pass along
Except for what a swan's produced.

And finally that true swan song
That one so simple, yet too long
About the wind beneath your wings
Won't seem so obviously wrong.

So every time Bette Midler sings
About the shadow her wing brings
I think of swans and gas and things
I think of swans and gas and things.

My Pain is Worse than Yours

Describe the deepest hopeless loss
The kind that gives your heart a toss
That seems to empty out your soul
And penetrates from core to gloss.

Image that you once were whole
Now nothing, nothing, can console
Your wounded spirit's beaten low
Your misery's beyond control.

Consider what it's like to know
That fate has dashed you to and fro
That now your suffering's complete
No refuge, none, where ere you go.

All this will pale in weak deceit
Compared to my replete defeat
When thoughtlessly I've pushed "delete"
When thoughtlessly I've pushed "delete".

The Cat

The cat who claws my garbage sack
Is tawny, neither grey nor black,
She gives scant notice to my cry
Her only thought to find a snack.

We've played this rit'al, she and I
A million times, or more, I sigh,
I've knelt among the orange peels
And other junk she's scattered by.

I guess you know how bad it feels
To live so close to one who steals
And leaves behind unholy mess
With every of her purloined meals.

I never fail, as I assess
The level of her last success
To offer words that fail to bless
To offer words that fail to bless.

The Sink

The dishes piled in the sink
A hazy mind that will not think
And speech that's really only mutter
All signs of someone on the brink.

Resolve as soft as summer's butter
And shadows rippling through the
shutter
Despondency is in the air
And settles in amidst the clutter.

The frozen will to offer prayer
Insentience in a vacant stare
A dripping faucet, burned out lights,
All signs of someone in despair.

A writer's heart that never writes
An acrobat, afraid of heights
And daylight swallowed up by nights
And daylight swallowed up by nights.

Some Singers

Some singers sing with angel choirs
And other chirp like birds on wires
Some howl like coyotes in the wild
At other singers and their fires.

Some singers have a tone that's mild
That sooths both mother and the child
While others chant both harsh and hot
Strong rhythms crazy and beguiled.

Some sing for dancers on a yacht
A dreamy sort of song, that's bought
Some croon for no one in the bath
Pretending they've a voice that's taught.

Some sing their little songs like math
All reckoning, no love or wrath
I hope my song's not on that path
I hope my song's not on that path.

The Troublehound

The troublehound sniffs everywhere
For wrecks and evil things to share
He isn't fooled by what looks right
No matter what, he shouts "Beware!"

The troublehound looks left and right
For every sign of wrong or blight
His motto isn't "all is well"
It's "every day's a coming night".

The troublehound will happ'ly tell
Of plots to take us all to hell
He sees the grey in every cloud
And tidal waves in every swell.

There's troublehounds in every crowd
They're never timid, always loud,
And every failure makes them proud
And every failure makes them proud.

She left her purse behind again

She left her purse behind again
The thousandth time since she turned ten
And had to change her shirt at noon
Because she spilled her ketchup then.

She can't recall her fav'rite tune
She sometimes butters with her spoon
Her car gets lost in parking lots
She decorates in early 'strewn'.

Her taps and crystal shine through spots
Her hairstyle features careless knots
And when she ever tries to cook
She's sure to overboil her pots.

And most the time if you will look
She's settled in a cozy nook
With heart and soul inside a book
With heart and soul inside a book.

They Just Delisted all My Stock

They just delisted all my stock
It didn't come much as a shock
To have my savings disappear
I'm use to having things in hock.

I pause and sniff, and shed a tear
These grieving times for me are dear
I've seen them come, then come again
Adversity is always near.

They say it's useless to complain
And bitter feelings entertain
Far better to move on than stay
A friend to grief, heartbreak and pain.

But since I'm such an easy prey
And steady target for harm's way
I've learned to glory in dismay
I've learned to glory in dismay.

Finish Line

You think there is a finish line
An end, a goal, a box of pine
You want a place to stop and rest
You want an end, you want a sign.

You feel you've done your very best
And surely passed this earthly test
And so you yearn for closure to
Your lifelong work, your endless quest.

Oh yes, a finish line will do
To make you feel your struggle's through
But nothing ever ends that neat
Some other race still waits for you.

And though an end may look quite sweet
Your racing's really not complete
The finish line is pure deceit
The finish line is pure deceit.

I Want a Sword in my White Cane!

Some people like their burgers plain
And keep their feet dry in the rain
But I like things more fun than that
I want a sword in my white cane!

Some people always smell a rat
Strain gleefully at every gnat
But I'm the sort that deals in trust
I like a bulldog, not a cat!

Some people will not eat the crust
A life of ease, for them's a must
But I prefer to chew on things
I'll never parry, always thrust!

Some people take just what life brings
They're pawns to governors and kings
They'll never know how my heart sings
They'll never know how my heart sings.

I Cannot Let a Poem Go By

Sometimes I hate to guess the way
These words, trite silly games at play,
Will tease the earnest reader's mind
And hide much more than they betray.

Come on! They tempt you. Try to find
What is it that they've left behind
A joy, a thought, a puzzled look?
Maliciousness or something kind?

So sometimes I won't even brook
The task of reading such a book
Pretending that the cost's too high
To comprehend the author's hook.

But in the end, I usually buy
Although I'm never certain why
I cannot let a poem go by
I cannot let a poem go by.

Who Knew?

He was a noble bird I think
Too bad he chose that time to blink
A flyer ought to keep both eyes
Wide open! Never, never wink!

I'm sure it caught him by surprise
A tree between him and his prize
Hello??!! Who put that in my way?
Bad news for thems who drives or flies.

Still what may bring the bird dismay
Was happy chance for squirrels at play
Saved by the limb from awful fate
The furry rodent's still okay.

And double blessing on this date
A handsome meal for coyote's plate
A squirrel was bait for what he ate
A squirrel was bait for what he ate.

my teeth are not like your teeth are

i'm easy going, you're not so
you're quick and, well... i guess i'm slow
we each shoot different sides of par
you like the winter, i hate snow.

my teeth are not like your teeth are
nor is my pickup like your car
my finger print is mine alone
your style's acknowledged, mine's
bizarre.

your locks are wavy, i've a dome
your perfume's not like my cologne
i speak my mind while you do not
my dna is not your clone

but though we differ quite a lot
it doesn't make me overwrought
i'm pretty sure you can be taught
i'm pretty sure you can be taught.

The list of things I want to know

The list of things I want to know
Is on the steady side of grow
I want learn to scuba dive
And make and bake some philo dough.

I want the expertise to drive
An 18 wheeler 9 to 5
And see in dirt and rocks and sand
The things now dead but once alive.

I'd like to learn to understand
Latino immigrants at hand
I'd like to write a poem or two
With vision that's more grand than
bland.

But most of all I think it's true
With all that's gone of what I knew
I'd like to keep the things I do
I'd like to keep the things I do.

Coulda Been 4 Bean Salad But it Wasn't

Green olives on your spoon at night
A gastric shock but sure delight
You lean the fridge against your head
And know this cannot turn out right

Then stumble back towards the bed
Insensitive and almost dead
You find your warm nocturnal nest
The covers covering your dread

The craving conquered with such zest
Won't offer any more protest
Against the sandman's gracious swoon
And so you slip into your rest.

Green olives singing out their tune
No longer rolling in your spoon
They're part of you, you silly loon
They're part of you, you silly loon.